U Boat

Shipping Losses Along the
Wigtownshire Coast in
the First World War

U Boat

Shipping Losses Along the Wigtownshire Coast in the First World War

By Julia Macdonald

Published by
G C Books Ltd
Unit 10 Book Warehouse
Bladnoch Bridge Estate
Wigtown
DG8 9AB
gcbooks@btinternet.com
www.gcbooks.co.uk

ISBN 978 1 872350 54 7

Layout and design by Michael Clayton
mj.clayton@btinternet.com

Printed by
J&B Print
32a Albert Street
Newton Stewart
DG8 6EJ

Contents

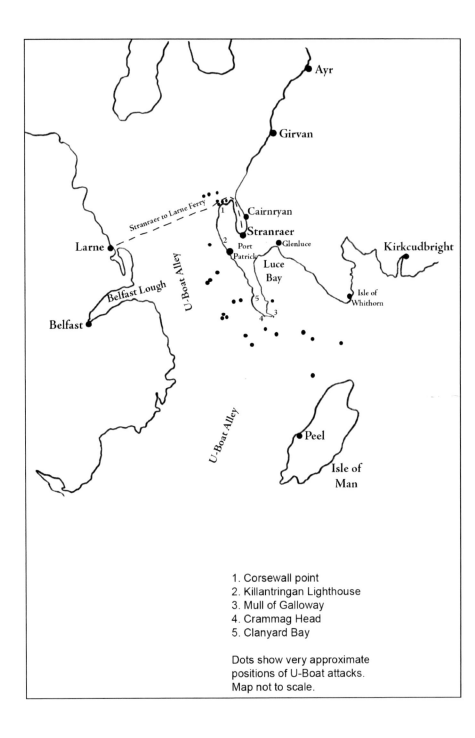

1. Corsewall point
2. Killantringan Lighthouse
3. Mull of Galloway
4. Crammag Head
5. Clanyard Bay

Dots show very approximate
positions of U-Boat attacks.
Map not to scale.

Introduction

Corsewall Lighthouse, like other lighthouses around the Wigtownshire coast, stands looking outward over a sea that hides beneath it the remains of many ships and their crews. Some of these vessels came to grief as a result of storm, collision or the unforgiving rocky shoreline, but during the First World War the busy seas around Wigtownshire proved a tempting area for German submarines to lie in wait for their prey. The North Channel in the Irish Sea became known as 'U-Boat Alley'.

Although the threat was difficult to spot from the sea, traces of the U-boats were more readily spotted from the air. Good defences for home waters were needed, but available aeroplanes were essential as accurate bombers at the Front. It was up to the Naval Admiralty to find an answer to defend the home waters and that answer was found in airships which were able to fly for relatively long periods of time. The Admiralty commissioned the construction of these somewhat experimental and flimsy aircraft as submarine scouts. An airship base was very quickly established at Luce Bay on the Wigtownshire coast early in 1915 to counter the U-boat threat and later the same year a mooring station was established on the other side of U-Boat Alley at Whitehead, County Antrim.

This book gives examples of the losses of some of the vessels attacked in the sea around Wigtownshire. In the year 1917 to 1918 alone there were at least a further 23 ships reported being damaged or chased, but the crews had escaped unharmed and the vessels reached a safe harbour. Most of those mentioned in the following pages rest now in silence on the sea bed.

The War at Sea

Britain had evolved into a prosperous empire throughout Queen Victoria's reign and the Industrial Revolution. She was one of the richest and strongest nations in the world, her position was enviable and while more than a few countries befriended her, others had plans to build their own empires to rival her. Powers such as Germany were expanding their armies while other countries planned revenge for previous humiliating defeats in battle.

Tensions had risen over a number of years between the continental countries and it took one seemingly minor event, the assassination of one man, Archduke Franz Ferdinand on 28th June 1914 to spark a war. Neighbouring countries immediately took sides, there was an opportunity for old scores to be settled and political alliances could be made, renewed or broken. Although most of the general public thought the war would be quickly over, this one event triggered a horrendous war on a scale never seen before which resulted in the death or permanent injury to more than thirty million men, women and children.

When war did break out, Britain had a very powerful navy. Her Grand Fleet was based at Scapa Flow in Orkney, a strategic position which would allow trade to continue with her colonies whilst seriously damaging German overseas trade and industry supply. She had little intention of using a massive army to fight on the continent, preferring to leave the protection of Europe to her early allies France and Russia. Many thought a decisive sea battle would end hostilities and early in the war large scale sea battles did take place, with many lives lost. None though, were decisive enough to win the war for either side.

German postcard demonstrating the hero status of U-Boat crews. Illustrated London News.

Although history claims that an attempt was made to use a submarine in an attack against a British ship in 1776, it was 1900 before the dual propulsion engine was introduced. This meant a combustion engine was used whilst the vessel was on the surface and an electric motor was used whilst the submarine was submerged. Quickly, in their quest for glory, many countries put this new design into production and by the outbreak of war it is thought that there were around 400 submarines worldwide.

Unterseeboot – UC Class submarine introduced in 1915 was mainly involved in mine laying duties. Postcard from the Author's collection.

In 1914 Germany had about 20 U-boats around a quarter of which were beset by difficulties which were often due to mechanical failure or human error rather than enemy action. The submarines varied in size and crew numbers, with smaller vessels having as few as a dozen men and larger vessels containing around 80. There were various classes of U-boats: coastal and ocean minelayers, coastal and ocean torpedo attack boats, with only a few merchant and cruiser U-boats. All were armed in some way, larger vessels could have as many as 24 torpedoes, most had deck guns, and others only the mines they laid. Torpedoes were generally well designed and only needed accurate aim to meet their targets however they sometimes did not contain enough explosive to sink the target quickly. Torpedoes also left a trail of bubbles which could allow the intended target time to swiftly change course.

The first British submarine was not launched until 1902. The submarines were very complicated to operate and the hand-picked volunteers who crewed them faced long periods of training.

Being a submariner was a prestigious but dangerous occupation – the vessels were often trapped in nets, mined or rammed, more often than not with the loss of all hands. By the end of January 1915 Germany had lost seven submarines, but the building of many new and better vessels had begun in earnest. British submarines did little better as during the course of the war they lost or seriously damaged at least 15 submarines in accidents rather than enemy combat. On one dreadful night during an exercise on the 31st January 1918 at Scapa Flow, five British submarines were involved in collisions where two vessels were lost taking the lives of over 100 submariners.

The use of submarines on both sides should have meant surprise attacks, however the rules of engagement at the onset of war meant that attacking vessels could only stop other ships and inspect their papers. If the ship was deemed an enemy, then passengers and crew would be allowed to gather their belongings and escape on lifeboats. Captured vessels could then be taken as a prize or sunk. Any advantage submarines had in terms of stealth was lost as they had to show themselves and demand papers.

Germany had declared the seas around Britain a war zone and had begun sinking merchant shipping faster than replacements could be built. Commanders of U-boats gained almost celebrity status and were hailed as heroes in their home country where they were bestowed with medals, and honours. Even Commanders of British ships were somewhat in awe of the ability, force and speed of the U-boat crews.

British shipyards were operating at maximum strength building merchant vessels and ships for defence, but it was not fast enough as they had taken heavy losses. The British Admiralty made the decision to defend merchant vessels and passenger ships with some force. As a result of this decision early in 1915, the rules of engagement changed, U-boats could attack armed vessels without prior warning.

The only way of successfully defeating a U-boat was to ram it at considerable risk to the attacking vessel or use depth charges to force it to surface near an armed vessel which could use large guns to sink it. If a vessel was known to be armed it was unlikely the submarine would surface.

Towards the end of 1914, after suggestion by Winston Churchill, the British began fitting out small vessels for use as Q-ships. These were heavily armed vessels with hidden guns disguised as innocent merchant vessels. As the U-boats could not attack unarmed vessels without prior warning, the plan was to lure the U-boat to the surface to demand papers, whereupon the Q-ship would suddenly drop the disguise and attack.

English survivors just before rescue by a German U-boat.

Within living memory of those in Britain, previous wars had all been fought in distant lands, with little awareness at home of the enormous loss, sacrifice and atrocities war could bring. Men volunteered happily in their thousands, for a war where they all expected to return home victorious by Christmas. Wigtownshire had one of the highest percentages of volunteers per head of population in the country. It was seen as an adventure where brothers, pals and neighbours enlisted together and sadly many of those men would never return home.

For almost a century Glenluce cemetery has been the final resting place for three unknown sailors from the Great War. Two are from the 'Main', a Welsh colliery ship which was sunk in Luce Bay with the loss of twelve lives.

The *Bayano*

As the families in the rural towns and villages of Wigtownshire continued to send their men to a war in far off lands, the conflict was brought to their doorstep with the sinking of the *Bayano* in 1915.

Little is mentioned or documented of the sinking by German U-27 of the naval auxiliary ship SS *Bayano* a few miles from Corsewall Point. With the loss of 196 lives it was the single largest loss of life these shores have ever seen.

The *Bayano* was a twin screw fruit and passenger steamer of around 6000 tons, built by Alexander Stephen & Sons (Ltd) in 1913. When launched the modern ship, owned by Elders & Fyffes (Ltd), provided first class accommodation and staterooms, insulated cold storage for fruit transport, wireless telegraphy and submarine signalling apparatus. She was to service the route between Bristol, the West Indies and Central America and was one of a fleet of ships known as 'Banana Boats'.

Postcard from the Author's collection.

The *Bayano* became a Royal Navy Auxiliary Cruiser in the early stages of the war. Though many of the crew were Scots, others came from around the UK, the Isle of Wight, and Isle of Man and as far away as Newfoundland. Some of the stokers had only just been employed before her fated trip and had previously only worked ashore.

U-27 was a formidable force to be reckoned with. Commissioned in May 1914 the submarine was built by Kaiserliche Werft, Danzig. Kapitän-Lieutenant Bernd Wegener had become well known in Germany and in Britain for his success in sinking other ships.

When the *Bayano* set out from the Clyde to take on coal at Liverpool on 11th March 1915 she had 222 men aboard. Under the command of Captain Henry Cecil Carr and in the darkness of the early hours the ship sailed in calm water past Ailsa Craig and by 5am she was around three miles off Corsewall Point. When the attack came, the majority of the men including the commander, were off-duty and sleeping in their bunks.

The force of the first explosion threw Captain Carr from his bunk and in the time it took him to throw on his great coat and rush to the deck he was already almost knee deep in the chilling water of the Irish Sea. The wireless operator Walter D S Lloyd was also off duty and hastily made his way through rising water to his post at the instrument room to help send SOS signals.

Postcard from the Author's collection. The inscription on the reverse reads "In remembrance of the 'Bayano', that Father was on the 11th March, that was torpedoed off Scotland."

Some of the lifeboats were badly damaged in the explosion and could not be used. Though there was very little time, an attempt was made to lower at least two of the lifeboats. The life-rafts, made of wood and copper and designed to float from the deck in an emergency were all tied and there was little chance for crew to cut through the ties and release all of them. Only two were released.

It seemed the calmness of the sea meant that although there was a sense of urgency in leaving the ship, no-one panicked. Those on duty donned life-belts and set about distributing them to the many others who rushed to the deck. About a minute or so after the initial impact, the boilers exploded. It was said no-one jumped overboard until the ship was at such an angle that sailors were leaping into the water faster than they could be counted. Captain Carr who had been handing out life-belts, ordered crew members to save themselves then returned to meet his fate at the bridge of his vessel. Some of those who had been on deck, lost their footing and found themselves plunged into the water and sucked down with the vortex.

John Campbell, George Graham and Donald Murray lost their lives.
Photographs courtesy of Guido Blokland at facememorialblogspot.com

The ship sank bow first within just three minutes of the boiler explosion. Those below deck did not stand a chance. The propeller lifted high out of the water before the ship slipped downwards and out of sight. Men and wreckage were strewn all around the area. The men could only see those closest to them as each man struggled in the bitter cold clutching to life on any piece of floating debris they could. Ten minutes after the ship went down the conning tower of U-27 was seen inspecting the wreckage. More time went by and the cries in the dark became silent as one by one men lost their struggle for survival. The remaining men knew what the silence meant. Those who could swam towards the two life-rafts and an upturned lifeboat. One hundred and ninety six men perished.

As daylight came the 26 survivors had drifted some distance on their two rafts. As they saw no other boats or rafts around them they feared they were the only survivors. All were suffering the effects of exposure – bruised and blood-stained; a few were more seriously injured. Nearly all were naked or wearing night-clothes and had been soaked through. The daylight meant the sailors could see the coast a few miles off and they made several attempts to right the upturned boat with the intention of rowing towards the shoreline. Fatigue and cold meant their attempts were unsuccessful.

The 'Bayano' in wartime livery as a Royal Navy Auxiliary Cruiser. From the Author's collection.

The *Balmarino* left Belfast around 5am and headed for Ayr under the command of Captain James Foster.   About eight miles South-West of Corsewall Point at around 8.30am they saw an upturned boat and two rafts of men waving rags to attract their attention.

Moving the exhausted and injured men from the rafts to transfer to the *Balmarino* took considerable time.   Captain Foster feared that

The rescue vessel 'Balmarino' © Courtesy Tony & Gwenllian Jones.

some of the men were so weak they would be dead within half an hour if they could not be removed from the raft to warmth and food. Having transferred most of the men aboard, the armed vessel *Tara* came on the scene and recovered those remaining. The *Balmarino* headed for Ayr, while the *Tara* sailed to Stranraer where survivors were given accommodation at the Kings Arms Hotel.

On board the *Balmarino* the rescued men were given dry clothes and warm food. The badly injured were also well tended to and all the men spoke very highly of the efforts Captain James Foster and his crew had made to rescue

Galloway Advertiser & Wigtownshire Free Press Photo. 'Bayano' survivors landed at Ayr.

them. On arrival at Ayr four men were taken to Ayr Hospital because of their injuries: Ernest Samuel Luck, Thomas George Rolfe, Dennis Taylor and Abner Whitcombe. The others were taken to Ayr Barracks and provided with quarters whilst the two rescued crew doctors found accommodation in the town's Station Hotel. Sadly, two of those rescued were killed later in the war.

The exact location of the wreck of the *Bayano* remains unverified. The rescue ship *Balmarino* was renamed *Ballybeg* in 1952 and was scrapped, aged almost 60 in 1957. The *Tara* was torpedoed and sunk on 5th November 1915 by U-35 off Sullum, an Egyptian port, with the loss of 12 crew members. Bodies and debris from the *Bayano* were recovered by the following vessels: *Norse*, *Dolores*, *Celesia*, and *Adventure*.

At the same time as the war had been brought to the Wigtownshire coast, the Battle of Neuve Chapelle had begun on the continent, with more shells being fired in the first hour than had been fired in the whole of the Boer War.

Hartdale

Two days after the *Bayano*, the same submarine struck again. U-27 torpedoed the British steamer *Hartdale* off the Mull of Galloway. *Hartdale* was built in 1910 by Craig Taylor & Son, Stockton. Operated by the Trechmann Steamship Company, she had earlier left Glasgow and was carrying coal. The ship had been chased down by U-27 for over an hour before the submarine had the opportunity to strike. Although the torpedo hit the target, the ship did not sink immediately. Perhaps feeling some remorse at the enormous loss of life on the *Bayano*, Kpt. Wegener had surfaced his submarine, warned of his presence and gave every chance to abandon ship before sending his torpedo. Most of the *Hartdale* crew heeded the warning and lowered lifeboats to make their escape. Two men were killed when they fell into the water and could not be rescued. A further three crew members, including the master Captain Martin, remained at their posts until the torpedo hit, before jumping into the water. The instant the ship was struck, an enormous plume of water and coal were thrown into the air.

The nearby Swedish steamer *Heindel* picked up the survivors who had made it to the lifeboats even though they were at risk of being sunk. Again Wegener did not immediately attack. He demanded the ship's papers which confirmed she was from a neutral country and then let her go unharmed.

Only two days earlier Wegener had chased rescuers away from the men struggling for survival when he had torpedoed the *Bayano*. This time he soon realised the last three men who had jumped into the water were likely to drown. He had already sent the Swedish rescue vessel on her way. Whatever his reasons, this time he turned rescuer, plucking Captain Martin, the First Mate and Chief Steward King from the water. The men on the lifeboats feared they would never see their comrades again since stories of previously captured sailors had not ended well.

Newspapers reported with amazement that after a period of questioning, Wegener supplied them with hot drinks, blankets and a bottle of brandy before transferring them to small boats. Wegener seemed genuinely disappointed that *Hartdale* was only carrying coal. He had wanted to target government supply ships.

However chivalrous his behaviour was during this rescue, the submarine continued its deadly patrol and is thought to have been responsible for sinking at least 30,000 tons of shipping.

Though not a local incident, the fate of U-27 became infamously known as 'The Baralong Incident', causing political outcry from Germany as the British Admiralty did not confirm the sinking immediately.

On 19th August 1915, Kpt. Wegener of U-27 had just sunk the White Star Liner *Arabic* and captured the *Nicosian* which it was thought he intended to scuttle. There were six German sailors who boarded *Nicosian* to ensure the ship was evacuated. HMS *Baralong* was a disguised Q-ship sailing under the American flag. Responding to calls for help originally from the *Arabic*, she approached the scene of the *Nicosian* where she ran up flags requesting permission "to save life only". Kpt. Wegener of U-27 immediately granted this request totally unaware of the real intent of the armed ship. When *Baralong* was almost upon the U-boat the disguise was dropped and she fired on the submarine which very quickly sank. As German sailors swam to be rescued they came under a hail of gunfire. Germans on board the *Nicosian* were found and executed. There were no German survivors. It was argued by some that this was a war crime, though others disagreed.

Cameronia

The Anchor Line vessel *Cameronia* had been sailing from New York to the Clyde when on 15th March 1915 as she was sailing past the Mull of Galloway, a submarine was spotted. *Cameronia* sailed at full speed in a zig-zag fashion and as she did so it was claimed her lookout spotted another two submarines giving chase. On this occasion she made it safely to the Clyde. Later in the war *Cameronia*, serving as a troop ship, was torpedoed and sunk in the Mediterranean.

Anchor Line 'Cameronia' (I) © reproduced with permission Norwayheritage.com

Former Sandhead resident Dr Smellie was amongst the survivors. He had been in his surgery on board when the ship was struck by torpedo, but he was unhurt. He went to the bridge where he remained with the captain and other officers until the ship went down. Having been plunged into the sea, he was rescued within half an hour by a destroyer which transported him to Malta. He was then returned home to recuperate.

U-boats were not reported attacking ships around Wigtownshire for some months after this incident. The war was raging elsewhere however and one of the most infamous losses at sea happened during this period. It was the incident which turned public opinion fully against Germany and was credited with increasing American support for the Allies. The *Lusitania* was sunk on 7th May 1915 off Old Head of Kinsale, Ireland, with the loss of almost 1200 lives.

The same week the Rev. A Murray Macgregor mentioned the sinking of the Lusitania in his dedication to Lieut. Archibald Gifford Moir, who had lost his life during the course of the second Battle of Ypres. Archibald was the first man to be killed in the war from Cairnryan Parish.

Ivrig, Dora, W D Potts, Helen

It was almost two years after the *Bayano* and *Hartdale* incidents before there was another submarine attack of any significance around the Wigtownshire coastline. The outcry at the huge loss of life with the sinking of *Lusitania* off Ireland in May 1915 meant Germany restricted its submarine attacks temporarily. The German effort became even more concentrated on merchant vessels in an attempt to stop essential supplies between Britain, the United States and the Allies. The losses continued to rise steadily as the toll of ships being sunk by German submarines in the war doubled between 1915 and 1916 to almost 1500. America entered the war in 1917, and the largest losses of shipping in the war at sea were in that year. Germany resumed unrestricted submarine warfare.

If the people of Wigtownshire had developed a false sense of security from the lack of war activity in the seas around them, they were to get a loud wake-up call in May 1917.

The Mull of Galloway, a favourite U-boat hunting ground. Postcard from Author's collection.

21

Built in 1891 the triple mast sailing ship *Marguerite Elise* went through a number of name changes before becoming the Norwegian sailing ship Ivrig. On 1st May 1917, whilst sailing from Dublin, the ship was captured ten miles south-west of Portpatrick. The captor was UC-65 under the command of Otto Steinbrinck. The whole crew of *Ivrig* were able to escape safely before watching their vessel being sunk by gunfire.

Otto Steinbrinck and the crew of UC-65 were to have a busy day, capturing *Dora* around 11 miles west of the Mull of Galloway. Then two more small vessels, *W D Potts* and *Helen* were also captured and scuttled in the same area. In each case the crew was allowed to disembark safely before watching their vessels sink.

Taizan Maru

The following day UC-65 continued to pick off any passing vessel with great success. *St Mungo* and *Derrymore* were sunk off County Down. Later the Japanese operated steamer *Taizan Maru*, carrying iron ore, was sunk eleven miles West of the Mull of Galloway. Otto and his crew then sank another three vessels that day.

The teaming of Otto Steinbrinck and UC-65 was a successful one; sinking around 100 ships altogether. By the end of the war, in terms of number of ships sunk, Steinbrinck was the most successful U-boat commander. By the time UC-65 was torpedoed by a British submarine Otto had moved on to another command. Steinbrinck was much decorated for his success and he had gained the respect of other U-boat commanders. He went on to have a successful industrial career aided by his membership of the elite German SS. Having served in the Second World War he was arrested in 1945, tried at Nuremburg and sentenced to six years imprisonment. He became ill and died whilst serving his sentence.

Main

In 1915 the Royal Naval Air Service had established an airship base at East Freugh, known as RNAS Luce. The submarine scouting airships patrolled the area over the sea, readily able to spot the tell tale feather-like wake of a periscope trailing through the water. The airships were armed with bombs, though their main purpose was to locate the position of submarines then call for help from Allied armed vessels. On a regular basis they gave escort to the Stranraer to Larne ferry *Princess Maud*.

RNAS Ground crew relax at East Freugh. From the collection of Donnie Nelson.

The *Main* was a defensively armed steamship hoping to settle overnight in Luce Bay on 9th October 1917. The crew of the *Main* may have felt secure in the knowledge that they would be protected by the presence of the Airship Station as they prepared for their evening stopover. Although they would perhaps have felt less secure had they known the amount of time the crew of the airships were spending in the local Garrick Hospital recovering from injuries caused by accident. The airships were of a flimsy construction and safe flights were often weather dependent. Manoeuvrability was difficult, often experimental and more hazardous than the threat any enemy could pose. Even the crew of the airship consisted of men who had volunteered for the Royal Naval Air Service knowing this new service was risky if not dangerous.

Artistically enhanced moonlit 1917 postcard of 'Princess Maud'. Postcard from the Author's collection.

RNAS Luce grew to employ around 170 personnel during the course of the war, and the local Garrick Hospital treated around 400 servicemen as in-patients over the same period, although not all those treated would be from the base or the cause of all admissions due to flight injuries.

Main had been built in 1904 by Mackie and Thomson Ltd, Govan. She was owned and operated by Main Colliery Co., Ltd., Cardiff. As darkness fell she was around one and a quarter miles East from Drummore. Lights of another vessel were seen approaching. Submarine UC-75 under the command of Johannes Lohs opened fire on the unprepared *Main*. The ship quickly sank with the loss of 12 lives. As daylight came Drummore residents did what they could to rescue survivors and recover the bodies. The Captain of the ship was found alive, though his own son was amongst those who died.

The *Main* was successfully salvaged by an Ardrossan company. By 1920 it was beached at Drummore to continue with repairs. On July 30th 1920 the general public were invited for the first time to come and view 'the havoc caused by U-boat torpedoes and gunfire'. Those who went to see her while she was being repaired paid a fee. By the time of the viewing of the *Main*,

The Garrick Hospital, Stranraer where RNAS personnel spent time recovering from injuries. From the Author's collection.

another ship, *Rio Verde*, had been sunk off the Mull of Galloway. A number of the men who lost their lives on the *Main* and on *Rio Verde* had been buried in Kirkmaiden churchyard and it was proposed that the monies raised from visitors to the ship would pay for a memorial in the churchyard. The sight of the ship for almost three years at Drummore had served as a constant reminder of those whose lives had been lost. *Main* returned to service in 1922.

In late 1917 the British Admiralty was becoming increasingly concerned about the morale of the British public when the weekly return was published showing the number of vessels being lost to U-boat attack. The decision was taken to suppress the weekly return, instead publishing a monthly report of the tonnage of shipping lost. This report took little account of damaged vessels which could be out of commission for some time to effect repairs.

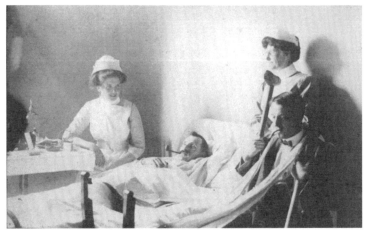

Injured RNAS personnel enjoy a smoking break in the Garrick Hospital. Photograph from the collection of Donnie Nelson.

Kirkmaiden Parish Churchyard. The inscription reads "In memory of our gallant merchant seamen of the steamers 'Main' and 'Rio Verde' who lost their lives by enemy action in Luce Bay and Crammag Head 1917. Erected by subscription from visitors boarding the salvaged steamer 'Main' while at Drummore, August 1920".

The wreck of *Main* could clearly be seen by locals in Drummore yet it went unreported in the local and national newspapers. Journalists were frustrated at being unable to record the news. *The Galloway Advertiser* and *Wigtownshire Free Press* reported:

> The submarine war is not going well...day by day one side of the picture which this war presents is being depicted and it is a glowing picture, but only once a month is a thing learnt of the campaign which the enemy is waging by sea.

The broadsheet sized newspaper had at least one column almost every week reporting local deaths whilst on service and a full page filled with photographs of the injured and missing, as well as those honoured with medals for bravery. Despite not being fully reported in newspapers, the close knit local community knew of the losses to shipping around their coast and were well aware that there was a possibility the war could be lost.

The Stranraer–Larne Ferry route

Though the Stranraer to Larne ferry *Princess Maud* was never directly attacked it is worth mentioning that she maintained the daily service under constant threat from submarine attack. It may never be known if she was an intended target, if it was simply luck or her speed, that her name is not included amongst those sunk or damaged.

One incident was simply an accident. On 10th January 1917 the very small vessel *Jura* was struck by the *Princess Maud* off the railway pier. *Jura* sank almost immediately.

The threat from submarines was thought to be increasing by 1917, so the steamer was defensively armed with a gun and gunners. She was regularly escorted by an airship from RNAS Luce Bay. The constant threat meant the service was occasionally suspended but this was rare as it was considered very important that the mail route would continue to operate without interruption.

The other local ferries, *Princess Victoria II* and *Princess May* had been commissioned for services by the Admiralty. *Princess Victoria* had a narrow

Photograph of the ferry being escorted up Lochryan, from the collection of Donnie Nelson.

escape from a torpedo whilst on the Dover to Boulogne route and returned unscathed to the Stranraer service at the end of the war. *Princess May* was based at Scapa Flow with the British fleet, providing accommodation for the many men stationed there. She was not to return to Stranraer and was scrapped in 1920.

Scene from around 1911 of the West Pier, Stranraer. Postcard from the Author's collection. The flagpole to the left of the pier was struck by an airship returning from escorting 'Princess Maud' in 1918. On this occasion the RNAS airmen escaped another stay in the Garrick.

'Princess Victoria II' was narrowly missed by torpedo whilst on the Dover–Boulogne
route during the war. Postcard from the Author's collection.

Princess Maud was fitted with wireless telegraphy and in 1918 her wireless
operator was a young man named David Broadfoot. On 31st January 1953
it was David Broadfoot who remained at his post sending distress messages
and signalling the position of the ill-fated *Princess Victoria IV*. The ferry
foundered in the mountainous seas during a great storm as she had taken
on water through her stern doors and lost engine power. The load on the
car deck had shifted and this made the vessel list heavily. Captain James
Millar Ferguson tried desperately to reverse the ship into the Loch but
the weather, combined with a lack of engine power, made the manoeuvre
impossible. Captain Ferguson, who had served as an officer in the Royal
Engineers in the First World War, initially thought the vessel was near
Corsewall lighthouse. Through continual signalling from David Broadfoot,
the vessel was later reported to be nearer Killantringan lighthouse, but they
seem to have been closing on the Irish coast.

Despite drifting close to the mouth of Belfast Lough, and her first signal
for help being sent out before 10am and the last radio signal just before 2pm,
she sank before help arrived. No women or children survived the tragedy as
neither of the lifeboats containing them withstood their launch from the
vessel or the huge sea swell. In all, 133 lives were lost with only 44 survivors.
A few of those who died had served in the First World War, more still had
survived the Second World War; some, like Broadfoot and Ferguson had
seen service in both wars and to die on what should have been a routine

short sea crossing was a dreadful tragedy. It was one of the worst maritime disasters in peacetime Scotland, yet it was never featured or mentioned in any part of a display in the Scottish Museum of Transport in Glasgow.

Both an initial inquiry and subsequent appeal found that the vessel was not fit to withstand heavy seas and was badly designed in the event of water flooding the car deck. David Broadfoot earned a posthumous George Cross which is on permanent display in Stranraer Museum. His grave is in Inch Churchyard, Castle Kennedy and is almost in an exact line with that of James Ferguson and two other officers who had remained at their posts as the vessel sank. There are monuments to those lost on the *Victoria* at both Stranraer and Larne.

The original position of the Victoria monument in Stranraer. The Stranraer monument was controversially moved in the mid 1990s with the redesign of Agnew Park.

The airships from RNAS Luce were not the only protection given to the Stranraer–Larne route. *Mona's Isle* had been part of the fleet of the Isle of Man Steam Packet Company; the paddle steamer was taken over by the Admiralty in 1915 and underwent a refit as an anti-submarine and net laying vessel. During the course of the war she called in to the port of Stranraer with some regularity.

The vessel worked mainly in the Irish Sea and her wireless operator in 1918 was Harold Bride. On the 15th April 1912, on board the White Star Liner *Titanic*, Harold, aged just 22, alongside Jack Phillips became the first men in history to send the new distress signal SOS. Harold was one of the few who survived but his feet were badly frostbitten. After *Titanic*, Harold left the Merchant Navy, however on the outbreak of war he volunteered and was returned to service as a wireless operator. The risk of sinking in *Mona's Isle*, a vessel in her twilight years, sailing on a daily basis in waters where U-boats regularly hunted, would have been far greater than the perceived safety of the 'unsinkable' *Titanic*, but the little paddle steamer proved her mettle defending the coastal waters throughout the war. Like *Princess May*

Postcard from the Author's collection of 'Mona's Isle'.

she was never to return to service as she too was scrapped at the end of the war. Harold Bride was famous, having appeared in newspapers across the world. The young David Broadfoot was yet to have his place in history. It seems almost incredible to think that the two wireless operators at one time lived less than 20 yards apart from each other in George Street, Stranraer and it is very possible they knew each other.

Postcard from May 1912. Harold Bride could remember the band playing as the ship plunged beneath the water. Postcard from the Author's collection.

In 1918, a charity football match between the crew of *Mona's Isle* and men from the Airship Station at RNAS Luce raised funds for the Garrick Hospital in Stranraer. Perhaps the monies raised helped pay for the increase in patient numbers from the Airship Station. Though it is not known if Harold Bride played in the match, it seems likely that he would have attended it and given his support.

After the war, Harold Bride married Lucy Downie in 1920 in Stranraer. Lucy was a teacher and taught at various local schools including Portpatrick, Glasserton and the old Academy. The couple had three children, all born in Stranraer or Kirkcolm. The Bride family had a number of homes locally including Kirkinner Manse.

Airship from RNAS Luce over Mosscroft Farm, Stoneykirk. Catherine McClelland watching. Miss McClelland (Author's Great Aunt), was a VAD nurse at Lochinch Castle during the Great War. She later became Mrs William McCulloch of High Mye Farm. Author's family photograph.

RNAS Ground Crew prepare a balloon for its next flight. The flimsy structure perhaps explains why the men spent much of their time in the Garrick Hospital. From the Donnie Nelson collection.

Harold continued his interest in wireless operations for many years. After the Second World War, a wireless listening station at the Isle of Whithorn welcomed a visitor one day who wanted to look around the station. He enjoyed tea and biscuits and was made very welcome, he became a regular visitor. It was only after Harold's death in 1956, in Stobhill Hospital, that his identity became fully known to the staff at the wireless station. Harold's wife Lucy returned to Stranraer after his death where she lived for many years at 17 Victoria Place.

Longwy

By 1917 the German U-boat fleet was now over 100 strong. While they had previously struggled to attack with any regularity on the West coast because of a shortage of long range submarines, this was now possible.

The French steamer *Longwy* had sailed from Spain under the command of Captain Joseph Huet. She was heading for the Clyde on 4th November 1917 and was around three miles North of Corsewall Point when she was attacked by UC-75 commanded by Johannes Lohs who had already sunk the steamship *Main* less than a month beforehand. Without warning, *Longwy* was struck by a torpedo and sunk. All 26 crew aboard perished and only three bodies were recovered when washed ashore near Girvan. Two of the men are buried in Doune cemetery, Girvan.

War Tune

On 9th December 1917, the American built *War Tune* was steaming from Barry, South Wales when around 1pm she was struck by torpedo without warning. Details are scant in the Admiralty returns and the loss is only included here because of the recording of the loss as being 1.5 miles from Black Head which could have been either Black Head in Belfast Lough or Black Head at Killantringan lighthouse. One crew member was killed.

U-53 was then under the command of Hans Rose, who in his own book of memoirs records that her load was unknown, although the Admiralty records it as coal.

Killantringan Lighthouse, Black Head Rock. Postcard from the Author's collection.

Three days earlier U-53 and Hans Rose had sunk the US destroyer *Jacob Jones* and had taken two badly injured American sailors aboard holding them prisoner and it was likely they were still aboard when *War Tune* was attacked. Since *Jacob Jones* was sunk off the south coast of Cornwall and a further ship, *Nyanza*, was damaged there by U-53 the day after *War Tune*, it is more likely therefore that the Black Head referred to is neither of those in the Irish Sea but is the one in Cornwall.

U-Boats versus HMS Lothbury

The Q-ship HMS *Lothbury* had once been the coal carrying and trading steamer *Argo*. On the morning of 27th December 1917, with Lieut. E Wilkinson in command, *Lothbury* and her 43 crew were half way between Point of Ayre, Isle of Man and Burrow Head, Isle of Whithorn. *Lothbury* thought she spotted two small fishing vessels in the distance. Within minutes of sighting the vessels, one appeared to be sailing straight for them, while the other had seemingly vanished.

Wilkinson quickly realised they were both enemy submarines. The approaching submarine opened fire on *Lothbury* who returned the fire

Lieut. E. Wilkinson. With kind permission Steve Robinson © Sea Breezes Magazine.

with her twelve-pound gun. While shrapnel rained down on *Lothbury*, they reported striking the submarine directly on the engine room. The submarine then took another direct hit at the base of their conning tower and was reported to take ten minutes to sink.

Lothbury then sailed to the site where the U-boat had gone down with the intention of gathering evidence of the sinking and to rescue some of the German sailors who were in the water. As she approached, the second submarine reappeared and fired. Wilkinson and his crew then claimed that the submarine was firing gas shells at them. As the *Lothbury* turned to return fire, the submarine fled the scene. Although Wilkinson gave chase and continued to fire, his vessel was not as fast as the submarine.

The crew of *Lothbury* struggled to defend themselves. During the battle they counted over 200 shots being fired at them from the munitions of the two submarines. The crew decided to use her smoke screens to prevent a clear view from the submarine if it should turn around again. At this point *Lothbury* was almost responsible for her own end. Whilst setting off the smoke screen a huge flame was sent in the air and she caught fire. Fortunately the fire was put out fairly quickly.

There were claims that the battle had been seen from the shores of both the Isle of Man and the Isle of Whithorn. As *Lothbury* had been fitted with wireless radio she had signalled for help from the outset. The battle was over when an Airship most likely from RNAS *Luce* appeared over the hills with HMS *Milbrook* arriving alongside the ship a few minutes later. As *Lothbury* sailed to relative safety the relieved crew were then reported to have relaxed by listening to gramophone records. Wilkinson then directed the vessel to anchor in Kirkcudbright Bay where the men were allowed ashore to celebrate.

The 'Argo' before she became the Q-Ship HMS 'Lothbury'. With kind permission Steve Robinson © Sea Breezes Magazine.

Wilkinson went on through the war receiving the Distinguished Service Cross, Lloyds Meritorious Service Medal, the Humane Society Medal, and the Order of the Crown of Italy. He also seems to have helped two airships in distress and was commended for his action in rescuing over 30 men. *Lothbury* was ordered to Milford Haven for a refit, although no serious damage had been incurred during the battle.

Amongst the listings of U-Boats lost during the First World War none seem to have been reported as lost on that date. Often ships would report hitting and sinking their target when in fact the target may have been damaged and could escape from sinking. Further, the report in this instance was written in 1920, almost three years after the incident and may have been exaggerated to make a good story for the Pacific Steam Navigation Company Magazine.

Smokescreen being set off to distract a chasing submarine. Illustrated London News 1919.

However it would seem very unlikely that the whole crew of a vessel would stick to the same story if it were not close to the truth. A letter signed by Vice Admiral Charles Henry Dare, on behalf of the Lord Commissioners of the Admiralty, commended Wilkinson and the crew of *Lothbury* for their actions when the incident was reported to them. Whilst the submarine may or may not have been sunk, *Lothbury* was a little ship crewed mostly by merchant seamen. She had beaten the odds admirably and counted herself lucky that she had not become another shipwreck and had survived to tell the tale.

Rio Verde

The losses to merchant vessels continued to rise. Many ships were being sunk on the Antrim coast around the Isle of Man and Ayrshire. It was suspected by many that whilst the campaign was going well abroad Britain was losing the war at sea. The cost of essential supplies such as food and clothing had risen sharply. The values of the cargoes being lost had been estimated in those days as hundreds of millions of pounds sterling.

Submarine Scout showing the flimsy structure of the aircraft and how exposed the pilots were to the elements. Illustrated London News March 1917.

On 20th February 1918 all flying from the airship base at East Freugh had been suspended for four days due to poor weather conditions. Helmut Patzig, the commander of U-86 took the opportunity to hunt in the unpatrolled seas around Wigtownshire. On 21st February 1918, the steamer *Rio Verde* with her cargo of coal was sailing from Glasgow with the intended destination of Milford Haven. As she passed Crammag Head, close to the Mull of Galloway she was torpedoed without warning. A few of the crew managed to struggle for survival in the chilled wintry sea and land at Clanyard Bay, though 20 of the crew were lost.

Five of those who died are buried in Kirkmaiden churchyard near the memorial to both *Main* and *Rio Verde*. A further grave, with no dates, is to an unknown sailor of the First World War.

Clanyard Bay where a few men scrambled ashore. Postcard from the Author's collection.

Kirkmaiden Churchyard, Five sailors from 'Rio Verde' and one unknown sailor rest either side of the memorial to both the 'Main' and 'Rio Verde'. Author's photograph.

RNAS Luce Bay, East Freugh. An airship shed was constructed in 1915, large enough to hold four airships. From the Donnie Nelson collection.

Ulabrand

The Norwegian steamship *Ulabrand* was steadily making her way towards the Clyde on 22ⁿᵈ February 1918. Close to the same spot where the *Rio Verde* had met her fate, at Crammag Head, the ship was struck. *Ulabrand* is likely to have hit a mine as no German submarine claimed responsibility. On impact the ship immediately began to list before quickly disappearing beneath the waves. In the darkness the men who were plunged into the water could not see each other but as daylight came 13 men had survived the night on a raft and a lifeboat. It is thought they were rescued and may have been brought ashore at Drummore.

Glass from the lighthouse at Crammag Head close to the Mull of Galloway. The small lighthouse was established in 1913 and was updated in 2009. Photograph courtesy of Edward Beck.

Haileybury

Built by Pickersgill & Sons, London in 1902 the *Haileybury* was run by a timber importing firm. She was on her way from Glasgow to France on 22ND February 1918 when she was struck by a torpedo about seven miles north-west of Portpatrick. There were two casualties, Captain James Clement Torkilson and Able Seaman John Livingston both lost their lives. *Haileybury* took nearly three hours to sink. The submarine U-91 was under the command of Alfred von Glasenapp.

After the war America wanted Glasenapp to be tried as a war criminal for his attacks on passenger liners. Amongst many other ships he was responsible for the sinking of the White Star Liners *Laurentic* and *Celtic*. Though there were no casualties on *Celtic*, 345 lives were lost from *Laurentic* off the north coast of Northern Ireland. As well as the tragedy of the number of lives lost, she was carrying millions of pounds worth of gold bullion to pay for the war efforts. The Government could not afford to lose this amount during the war and ordered the recovery of the gold. Though an extensive recovery operation retrieved most of the bullion, the salvage operation involved the use of explosives to blast an entry to the ship where she lay on the sea bed. This meant some of the gold could have been dispersed over a wide area as a considerable amount of the gold was never recovered.

Romeo

SS 'Romeo'. By kind permission Patricia McCormack, Immigrant Ships Transcribers Guild.

On 3rd March 1918 in the early hours of the morning, *Romeo* was steaming south of the Mull of Galloway when she was struck by a torpedo. The force of the explosion was so great that the ship immediately began to sink and was completely out of sight within two minutes. Only three of the 37 crew survived, John Compagnon, William Camomile and Arthur Seddon. Though *Romeo* was originally reported by the Admiralty as having been torpedoed ten miles off the Mull of Galloway, she lies 12 miles north-west of Peel, Isle of Man. She is mentioned here simply because of the original inaccuracy in reporting the place of her loss, though the error is only of a few miles. The letters from her name on her bow are in the Manx National Heritage collection.

Memorial postcard published on the death of Lord Kitchener. From the Author's collection.

U-102 commanded by Curt Beitzen was responsible for sinking *Romeo*. Beitzen was not as famous as other submarine commanders though he had previously commanded U-75 and had laid the mines around Scapa Flow that sunk HMS *Hampshire*. Six hundred and forty three men were killed including Field Marshall Horatio Herbert Kitchener. Only 12 men survived. Kitchener's body was never found. The most famous British military figure was dead. Beitzen and U-102 were lost close to the Orkney Islands in September 1918.

Destro

Destro was a fairly new British steamer having only been built in 1914 in Hull. She had been attacked previously by gunfire from a submarine in 1916. The captain, Edward Borrowdale Johnston had received a Distinguished Service Cross for his part in that action. He had managed to save the ship and his crew.

By March 1918, U-96 and Heinrich Jess were regularly waiting for ships around the Galloway coast and the Isle of Man. On 25th March around five miles south-west of the Mull of Galloway *Destro* came into the view of the submarine. This time *Destro* was struck by torpedo. Six men were killed and 15 others survived in a lifeboat. Initial Admiralty reports did not record any lives lost. As *Destro* sank, Heinrich Jess apparently directed the survivors to row towards Maryport Beach round the Mull.

Inkosi

Built in 1902 by Hall Russell in Aberdeen, the *Inkosi* was bound for Brazil under the command of Captain John Arthur. On 28th March 1918, three days after *Destro* was torpedoed and sunk, *Inkosi* was torpedoed by the same submarine, U-96 under the command of Heinrich Jess. She was around 10 miles south-west of Burrow Head. Three men were killed in the engine room. The ship did not sink instantly giving time for the remaining 48 crew to abandon the vessel. *Inkosi* drifted for a few miles before U-96 resurfaced and finished the job, sinking her with gunfire. The crew landed at the Isle of Whithorn where they were given accommodation for the night at the local school house. The entire action had been watched by locals from viewing vantage points on the Isle of Whithorn.

SS Inkosi, reproduced with kind permission © National Maritime Museum, Greenwich, London.

Solway Queen

Built in 1883 by R. Smith, Preston the steamer *Solway Queen* was operated by Kynoch-Arklow Ltd of Aberdeen. On 2nd April 1918 as she sailed from Ayr to Newry with a cargo of coal she was struck by torpedo about seven miles west of Black Head, within sight of Killantringan lighthouse, near Portpatrick. Eleven men including the master lost their lives. This time the submarine responsible was U-101 whose commander Carl Siegfried Georg was responsible for sinking hundreds of thousands of tons of merchant shipping during the course of the war.

Sister ship of Solway Queen by kind permission © Tony & Gwenllian Jones.

Lakemoor

The *Lakemoor* was on her maiden voyage across the Atlantic for her operators
the U S Navy. On board the new ship the crew were all naval reserves and
were commanded by Lieutenant Commander Kinchen J Powers. At around
midnight on 11th April 1918 as she headed for the Clyde with a cargo of
mines, she was torpedoed three miles north-west of Corsewall Point. The
enormous explosion was heard around the coast. Otto von Schrader with UB-
64 had been cruising the area looking for likely victims. The *New York Times*
reported 44 Americans killed. Fourteen of the surviving crew including the
Captain, landed at Dally Bay, a notorious place for ship wrecks just a few
miles south of Corsewall Point, but this time it was not the rocks that had
claimed the lives of their fellow sailors. The noise of the explosion brought
locals to the bay where they were able to offer aid to the stricken men.

Kafue

Built in 1913 by Palmer's Ship Building & Iron Co., in Newcastle, *Kafue* was carrying a general cargo. She had steamed along the Clyde and was well prepared for her long journey to Calcutta. On 30th April 1918 she was torpedoed with no warning 11 miles south-west of the Mull of Galloway. One crew member died. This time the submarine responsible was U-86 and the commander, Helmut Patzig.

Medora

U-86 continued to look for victims around the Mull of Galloway and just two days after *Kafue*, *Medora* came into view.

Built in 1912 as the *Frankmount* in Glasgow and owned by Canadian Pacific Railway Ocean Lines the steamer had a general cargo and was heading from Liverpool to Arran before intending to sail onwards to Montreal.

Medora was attacked in almost exactly the same spot as Patzig hit his previous target, 11 miles south-west of the Mull of Galloway. It was thought that the torpedo used in this case was light on explosives. The pilot of *Medora* was asleep in the chart room at the time the torpedo hit and there was insufficient noise from the impact to rouse him. There were no casualties and the crew evacuated themselves safely into the lifeboats.

The ship sank very slowly. The stories from survivors told of the submarine surfacing close to the lifeboats. Apparently Helmut Patzig demanded in a well-spoken English voice that the Captain, Wireless Operator and Gunner were delivered to his submarine immediately. The men bravely stood up, though the second gunner took the place of the first gunner by wearing his fellow officer's hat. The gunner was married with children and the second gunner was single.

The submarine then sent 20 shells into *Medora*, and sped off with the three prisoners. When they were about five miles distant Patzig was informed that *Medora* was still afloat. Furious he returned to the scene firing five more shots before *Medora* was finally defeated and sank stern first.

That day an armed British ship reported that they had gunned down and sunk a German submarine, though this was in the Strait of Dover. It was feared the British prisoners would all have been killed. It was later reported that it could not have been U-86 that had been sunk as the three captured crew members had been taken to a prison camp.

Another 'kill' by U-86 and Commander Helmut Patzig. The 'Covington' sinks slowly off Brest, France having been hit by two torpedoes without warning. She was returning home in 1918 having delivered essential munitions and supplies to the troops in France. Postcard from the Author's collection.

A lifeboat and two dinghies of shipwrecked sailors row towards a U-boat. Postcard from the Author's collection.

Patzig was wanted for war crimes after the war as he targeted and sunk the clearly marked hospital ship *Llandovery Castle* off the south coast of Ireland. Patzig and two other officers shot at crew, nurses and medical staff in lifeboats and those struggling in the water. There were only 24 survivors from the 258 on board. He fled to South Africa and was never brought to trial.

Sandhurst

The British steamer *Sandhurst* was built in 1897 and was owned by the British Steamship Company. On 6th May 1918 she had made the journey from Spain safely and was now in the Irish Sea about six miles off Corsewall Point heading for Ardrossan. She was struck by torpedo from UB-72 commanded by Friedrich Träger and sunk with the loss of all 20 on board.

Six days later UB-72, Friedrich Träger and all but three of his crew were killed by torpedo from HM Submarine D4. They had been pursued for some distance by the British submarine and by other ships dropping depth charges. She was damaged, leaking badly and leaving a trail of oil behind her. The submarine tried to make her escape through the Irish Sea and had been bombarded for hours. The trail of oil made her very easy to follow and she could not submerge because of the damage. She was close to Guernsey before meeting her fate.

Three days after UB-72 was sunk, Drummore coastguard reported spotting a submarine in Luce Bay. Airship patrols from the airship station, which had been renamed to become RAF Luce Bay, did not find any trace of the vessel.

Buffalo

The *Buffalo* was a relatively small vessel carrying coal owned by J Little & Sons, Saltcoats. On 13th September 1918, as she made her way from Ayr to Dundalk under the command of Master James Busby she was struck by torpedo from UB-64. The *Buffalo* was around seven miles north-west of Corsewall Point. All 10 crew on board were killed, none of their bodies were ever recovered.

Including *Buffalo* and *Lakemoor*, the submarine commanded by Otto von Schrader had destroyed around 28 ships. On the same day as UB-64 struck *Buffalo*, it successfully torpedoed another two vessels: the Belfast based *M J Craig* was sunk seven miles off Belfast Lough with the loss of four lives, and the *Setter*.

Setter

On 13th September 1918 the third vessel sunk by UB-64 in the one day was the defensively armed passenger steamer *Setter*. The ship operated by G & J Burns Ltd passed the mouth of Lochryan, about nine miles north-west of Stranraer, when Otto von Schrader's submarine attacked. All nine on board *Setter* perished.

UB-64 surrendered on 21st November 1918. Otto von Schrader was a much decorated Admiral who went on to serve through World War Two. He committed suicide in 1945.

Nyanza

Nyanza was built in 1897 by A Stephen & Sons, Glasgow. Although the same name as one damaged in 1917 by Hans Rose in U-53, it was not the same vessel. The steamer was torpedoed around 10 miles north-west from Corsewall Point on 29th September 1918. She was very unlucky as she was the only ship to be sunk by the newly built UB-95. All 13 men aboard Nyanza were lost.

By this date many people were contracting 'Spanish Flu'. The deadly epidemic was spreading around the world at some speed, its path hastened by the movement of troops and sailors from all the nations involved in the War.

Bonvilston

Operated by Douglas Hill Steam Ship Co Ltd Cardiff, the British defensively armed merchant ship Bonvilston was built in 1893 by Palmers Co Ltd Newcastle. In 1916, Bonvilston had accidentally collided with the transport ship HMAT Geelong in the Mediterranean, sinking her. On her final journey on 17th October 1918 Bonvilston was sailing from Ayr to her intended destination at Barry Roads, Glamorgan. The war was reaching an end as Germany had already requested an armistice with the Allies earlier that month. Some members of the German Navy were not happy at the armistice and were determined to try to demonstrate their might. Johannes Paul Müller had only been in command of UB-92 since July that year and may have had something to prove. Around nine and a half miles north-west by west of Corsewall Point a single torpedo struck the Bonvilston and she began to sink. Lifeboats were safely launched and all 26 of the crew escaped. UB-92 surrendered on the 21st November 1918 and was broken up at Bo'ness. Bonvilston was the last ship to be sunk around the Wigtownshire coast before armistice was declared.

The End of the First World War

Princess Maud passes Corsewall lighthouse around 1908. Postcard from the Author's collection.

On the 11th day of the 11th month at the 11th hour in 1918, armistice was declared. The Great War was over. After the celebrations of peace, thoughts turned towards honouring those whose lives had been lost. Memorial stones were placed on distant battlefields and in almost every cemetery or churchyard locally. For many whose lives were lost within sight of our shores, their names may never be known. Their final resting place marked only by the light cast over the water from the lighthouses on the Wigtownshire coast.

The U-Boats Return

U-Boats were to return to Lochryan during the Second World War. The hunting ground around the coast of Wigtownshire saw far fewer losses to merchant and armed shipping than had been seen in the Great War.

In 1945 U-Boats started their surrender and 86 were held at Cairnryan Military Port. The port was of great significance during the Second World War and was chosen alongside Faslane by the Government as the second port, should there be extensive bombing at Liverpool or Greenock. The intention was to ensure essential supplies from the United States of America could still reach the British mainland.

The captured German crew from the U-boats must have totalled a few hundred and became quite a spectacle as they were exercised nightly along Cairnryan Road. Normally the British officers in charge were from the Home Guard and were thought by locals to be no fit match for the elite, physically fit, and well fed looking German crewmen. Often the German submariners were taunted by boys from the railway worker's houses at Marine Gardens, who included the author's father and local historian, Donnie Nelson. The boys threw rocks or fired missiles from catapults.

The smiling crew of one of the surrendered U-boats awaiting inspection by a British Senior Officer. From the Donnie Nelson collection.

There was a large prisoner of war camp in the grounds of Sheuchan School Stranraer, but as the war was over there was little point in any of the prisoners escaping whilst they waited to be returned to their home country.

When the war was over the submarines were towed out to the Atlantic and scuttled in an operation known as Deadlight. Some U-Boats did not make it that far having broken from their tow and are rumoured to lie not far out of the mouth of Lochryan, in all 36 did not make it to their intended scuttling site. By the end of the year all the U-boats had left the Loch.

Submarines continued to be scrapped at Cairnryan up until around 1990, though by this time scrapping was much more conventional and did not involve dumping the vessels in deep water.

U-boats in Lochryan awaiting destruction after WWII. From the Donnie Nelson collection.

*Russian and Polish submarines waiting to be scrapped at Cairnryan around 1990.
From the Donnie Nelson collection.*

Paddle steamer passes by Corsewall lighthouse. From the Author's collection.

The Fate of the Great War U-boats

U-27 Bernd Wegener. Sank 11 merchant vessels and a warship. This total included the *Bayano* and *Hartdale*. Around a year after taking command of U-27, the submarine was sunk and the entire crew killed in the infamous Baralong incident.

U-53 Hans Rose. Sank 87 merchant vessels and one warship, badly damaged many other ships. The total includes *War Tune*. U-53 surrendered in December 1918. Rose had developed a strong reputation during the war of being a fair man in battle; ensuring survivors from the opposing side were given a better chance of being rescued. He wrote a book about his part in the war and had the artist Claus Bergen sail with him in U-53 capturing everyday events and battles on canvas. He went on to serve in the Second World War training the crew of U-boats.

U-86 Helmut Patzig. Sank 33 merchant ships including *Rio Verde*, *Kafue*, and *Medora*. The submarine was surrendered in November 1918. Patzig went on to serve in the Second World War.

U-91 Alfred von Glasenapp. Sank 37 merchant vessels including *Haileybury*. U-91 surrendered in November 1918 although America wanted Glasenapp tried as a war criminal there is little trace of what happened to him after the war.

U-96 Heinrich Jess. Sank 31 ships including *Destro* and *Inkosi*. U-96 surrendered in November 1918 while Jess died in 1958.

U-101 Carl Siegfried Ritter Von Georg. The U-boat sank 23 ships including *Solway Queen*. U-101 surrendered in November 1918. Von Georg was tried as a war criminal but acquitted, he died in 1957.

U-102 Curt Beitzen. The U-boat sank four ships including *Romeo*. U-102 was lost with all 42 crew including Beitzen around the end of September 1918, it is presumed the submarine hit a mine.

UB-64 Otto von Schrader. The U-boat sank 29 ships, damaged others and took one as a prize. The vessels sunk included *Lakemoor*, *Buffalo*, and *Setter*. UB-64 surrendered in November 1918. Schrader commanded other submarines and he was a part of the sinking of 67 vessels in the Great War. He went on to serve in the Second World War and was suspected of war crimes. It is believed he committed suicide in 1945 rather than surrender.

UB-72 Friedrich Träger. In only two months of command Träger had sunk four ships and badly damaged another including *Sandhurst*. Only six days after *Sandhurst*, Träger was killed alongside 34 of his crew when the British submarine D4 torpedoed the U-boat

UB-92 Johannes Paul Müller. The submarine sank a total of eight vessels including *Bonvilston* before being surrendered in November 1918, it is not known what happened to the commander.

UC-65 Otto Steinbrinck. While the U-boat sank 105 ships including *Ivrig*, *Dora*, *W D Potts*, *Helen*, and *Taizan Maru*, Steinbrinck had a grand tally of 206 ships sunk. UC-65 was sunk by torpedo from a British submarine in November 1917, but Steinbrinck had moved command. A successful industrialist, Steinbrinck was tried at Nuremburg for being a member of the elite SS and sentenced to six years in prison. He became ill having served almost two years of his sentence and died in prison.

UC-75 Johannes Lohs. The U-boat sank 58 ships including *Main*, and *Longwy*. UC-75 was sunk in 1918 but Lohs was not aboard as he had moved on to the command of another U-boat. He was one of the most successful commanders of the German U-boat fleet and was much decorated for his success having sank 76 vessels and damaged many more. However, eight months after he took his new command on UB-57, the submarine struck a mine and he was killed.

UB-95 Oskar Maass. The only vessel sunk by the U-boat and commander was *Nyanza*. At the end of the war UB-95 was surrendered and broken up, it is not known what happened to the commander after the war.

Bibliography

Books

Bell, Archie, *Stranraer in World War Two*, Stranraer and District Local History Trust, 2005

Coswill, Miles, *Stranraer–Larne, The Car Ferry Era*, Ferry Publications, Pembrokeshire, 1995

Grant, Robert M, *U-Boat Hunters*. Periscope Publishing, Penzance, 2003

Hallam, R. & Beynon, N, (eds) *Scrimgeour's Small Scribbling Diary 1914-1916*, Conway, London, 2008

MacHaffie, Fraser G, *The Short Sea Route*, Stephenson & Son, Merseyside, 1975

Miller, P C, *Galloway Shipwrecks*, Sunquest, Ardwell, 1992

Rose, Hans, *Auftauchen, Kriegsfahrten von U53*, Germany, 1939

Tennent, A J, *British Merchant Ships Sunk By U-Boat in World War One*, 1990

Warner, Guy, *Airships Over The North Channel: Royal Naval Air Service Airships in Ulster during the First World War*, Colourprint Books, Newtownards, 2005

Williams, M, *History of the Garrick Hospital 1892-1992*, Wigtown Free Press, Stranraer, 1992

Articles

Galloway Gazette
Illustrated London News, March 1917
New York Times
Scotsman
Starling Press, Gwent.
Stornoway Gazette, 1921
Wigtown Free Press

Websites

http://facememorialblogspot.com
http://1914-1918invisionzone.com
http://wrecksite.eu
www.archivesnetworkwales.info
www.cwgc.org
www.geocities.com/~orion47/ (website now closed)
www.gracesguide.co.uk
www.immigrantships.net
www.isle-of-man.com
www.isleofwhithorn.com
www.mercantilemarine.org
www.nationalarchives.gov.uk
www.naval-history.net
www.norwayheritage.com
www.rcahms.gov.uk
www.rhiw.com
www.roll-of-honour.com
www.seabreezes.co.im
www.uboat.net

Conversation and correspondence by letter, e-mail and telephone.

Elaine Barton, Archie Bell, Guido Blokland from Facememorial, Adrian Corkhill, Tony & Gwenllian Jones, Don Kindell & Gordon Smith at naval-history.net (where a full list of the casualties of the *Bayano* can now be viewed), Edward Beck, Patricia McCormack from Immigrant Ships Transcribers Guild, Morag Williams, Donnie Nelson, Mrs Nield and all the staff of Stranraer Library, Steve Robinson from *Sea Breezes Magazine*, Gudmundur Helgason at Uboat.net, and Børge Solem at Norway Heritage.

Photograph Acknowledgements

Author's collection, front cover and pages 3, 9 (bottom), 11, 12, 13, 14, 16 (top), 21, 24, 25, 26 (bottom), 28 (bottom), 29, 30, 31, 32, 33 (top), 35, 40, 44, 49, 50, 53, 56 (bottom)

Børge Solem at Norwayheritage.com page 20

Donnie Nelson collection pages 23, 26 (top), 28 (top), 33 (bottom), 41, 54, 55, 56 (top)

Edward Beck page 42

Galloway Advertiser and *Wigtown Free Press* page 17

Guido Blokland at facememorial.com, page 15

Illustrated London News page 9 (top), 38, 39

Immigrant Ships Transcribers Guild page 43 (bottom)

National Maritime Museum page 46

Steve Robinson *Sea Breezes Magazine* 36, 37

Tony and Gwenllian Jones page 16 (bottom), 47

Wikipedia page 43 (top)